Family

Scripture Study Journal

By Shannon Foster

D1621604

Volume ____

Number your journals starting with 1 in order to keep them organized

Date of First Entry _____

Date of Last Entry _____

For examples and tutorials on how to use this journal, come to:
www.theredheadedhostess.com

How to Use this Journal

- This journal is designed to aid you and your family in having a fun and effective scripture study.

- It is also designed to be a record of your family. If used daily, you will have records of your daily schedules along with things said, thought, and written.

- On page 3 is a Table of Contents to help you keep an organized record of what you studied.

- Below are some ideas on how you can use the Table of Contents

4-5	Matthew 1:1-10
6-7	Matthew 1:11-19 (July 6, 2012)
8-9	President Packer's talk, "Washed Clean"
10-11	Family Discussion on CHARITY

- Each page in the journal is designed for one day of family scripture study. It is designed so it can be done quickly in a 10 or 15 minute time slot or to be used for a longer reading or discussion. Encourage your children to do much of the writing in the journal. Not only will they feel more involved, but it is also a record of their handwriting as they grow older.

- **DATE, TIME, PLACE and WHAT IS HAPPENING IN OUR LIVES TODAY:**

  - "Date, Time and Place" is meant to be a snapshot of your family at the moment you begin your study. "September 3, 2012, 6:45 AM, the kitchen table" is an example of what you could write.

  - "What is happening in our lives today" is a snapshot of your family that day and what your comings and goings are going to be. "Dad is going to work, Mom is going to be room-mother in Anna's class, Kyle has a soccer game that we are all going to, and Rachel has a big test in math" is an example of what you could write.

- **IN ONE SENTENCE, TODAY WE ARE STUDYING:**

  - Here you can ask your children or explain to them what it is you are going to be reading about. It can look like this: "Christ is going to heal a blind man" or "What our family can learn from Christ healing a blind man".

  - You could also wait until after you finish studying and ask your children to come up with a sentence that describes what you studied.

- **THINGS WE NEED TO UNDERSTAND:**

  - This is where you can explain any background information before you begin studying to help your family have a greater perspective of what is going on.

  - This could include historical information, descriptions of people, cultural information, definitions, maps, etc.

- *After you have filled in the above sections, you would then read and discuss the scriptures together as a family and fill in the below sections when you have finished.*

- **WHAT WE LEARNED:**

  - This box is flexible to meet the needs of your family. Here are some ideas for you (however, you may want to come up with some of your own ideas):

  - **Draw a picture:** If you have children who cannot read or write, you can have them draw pictures of what you are studying in this box (wouldn't that be fun to look back at years later?).

  - **Write a list of principles and doctrines:** As you read, have your family search for and record principles and doctrines they find. For example: Verse 1 = faith in God, repentance brings happiness

  - **Draw a map:** If you are reading about a story or journey, draw it as you read verse by verse. Draw people traveling, camping, fighting, etc.

  - **Make a family motto:** If you read some scriptures that really apply to your family, make a family motto and write it really big in this space.

  - **Write down something someone said:** If, while you are studying, someone said something really insightful, write it in quotes in this space so it is recorded as a part of your family history.

- **FAVORITES:**

  - After you finish reading, have everyone share their favorite thing they read and why they chose that.

- **GOALS:**

  - In this box you can have everyone make a personal or family goal centered on what you learned that day. Example: "We will do a secret act of service for a family member this week".

Table of Contents

WHAT we are studying today

Date: _____   **Time:** _____   **Place:** _____

What is happening in our lives today:

_____

_____

_____

In one sentence, today we are studying:

Things we need to understand before we read:
(background information)

What we learned: (Draw a picture, write a list of principles and doctrines you found, make a diagram, draw a map, make a family motto, write one word to sum up what you learned, find and write a quote about what you studied, write down something someone in your family said while you were studying, have someone write their testimony about what you discussed, etc.)

Favorites:

Name	Favorite scripture, phrase or thing they learned today	Why they chose this

Goals: (What we can do to apply what we learned to our lives)

WHAT we are studying today

Date: _____   Time: _____   Place: _____

What is happening in our lives today:

_____

_____

_____

In one sentence, today we are studying:

Things we need to understand before we read:
(background information)

What we learned: (Draw a picture, write a list of principles and doctrines you found, make a diagram, draw a map, make a family motto, write one word to sum up what you learned, find and write a quote about what you studied, write down something someone in your family said while you were studying, have someone write their testimony about what you discussed, etc.)

Favorites:

Name	Favorite scripture, phrase or thing they learned today	Why they chose this

Goals: (What we can do to apply what we learned to our lives)

WHAT we are studying today

Date: _____ Time: _____ Place: _____

What is happening in our lives today:

_____

_____

_____

In one sentence, today we are studying:

Things we need to understand before we read:
(background information)

What we learned: (Draw a picture, write a list of principles and doctrines you found, make a diagram, draw a map, make a family motto, write one word to sum up what you learned, find and write a quote about what you studied, write down something someone in your family said while you were studying, have someone write their testimony about what you discussed, etc.)

Favorites:

Name	Favorite scripture, phrase or thing they learned today	Why they chose this

Goals: (What we can do to apply what we learned to our lives)

WHAT we are studying today

Date: _____   Time: _____   Place: _____

What is happening in our lives today:

_____

_____

_____

In one sentence, today we are studying:

Things we need to understand before we read:
(background information)

What we learned: (Draw a picture, write a list of principles and doctrines you found, make a diagram, draw a map, make a family motto, write one word to sum up what you learned, find and write a quote about what you studied, write down something someone in your family said while you were studying, have someone write their testimony about what you discussed, etc.)

Favorites:

Name	Favorite scripture, phrase or thing they learned today	Why they chose this

Goals: (What we can do to apply what we learned to our lives)

WHAT we are studying today

Date: _____   **Time:** _____   **Place:** _____

What is happening in our lives today:

_____

_____

_____

In one sentence, today we are studying:

Things we need to understand before we read:
(background information)

What we learned: (Draw a picture, write a list of principles and doctrines you found, make a diagram, draw a map, make a family motto, write one word to sum up what you learned, find and write a quote about what you studied, write down something someone in your family said while you were studying, have someone write their testimony about what you discussed, etc.)

Favorites:

Name	Favorite scripture, phrase or thing they learned today	Why they chose this

Goals: (What we can do to apply what we learned to our lives)

WHAT we are studying today

Date: _____ **Time:** _____ **Place:** _____

What is happening in our lives today:

_____

_____

_____

In one sentence, today we are studying:

Things we need to understand before we read:
(background information)

What we learned: (Draw a picture, write a list of principles and doctrines you found, make a diagram, draw a map, make a family motto, write one word to sum up what you learned, find and write a quote about what you studied, write down something someone in your family said while you were studying, have someone write their testimony about what you discussed, etc.)

Favorites:

Name	Favorite scripture, phrase or thing they learned today	Why they chose this

Goals: (What we can do to apply what we learned to our lives)

WHAT we are studying today

Date: _____   Time: _____   Place: _____

What is happening in our lives today:

_____

_____

_____

In one sentence, today we are studying:

Things we need to understand before we read:
(background information)

What we learned: (Draw a picture, write a list of principles and doctrines you found, make a diagram, draw a map, make a family motto, write one word to sum up what you learned, find and write a quote about what you studied, write down something someone in your family said while you were studying, have someone write their testimony about what you discussed, etc.)

Favorites:

Name	Favorite scripture, phrase or thing they learned today	Why they chose this

Goals: (What we can do to apply what we learned to our lives)

WHAT we are studying today

Date: _____   Time: _____   Place: _____

What is happening in our lives today:

_____

_____

_____

In one sentence, today we are studying:

Things we need to understand before we read:
(background information)

What we learned: (Draw a picture, write a list of principles and doctrines you found, make a diagram, draw a map, make a family motto, write one word to sum up what you learned, find and write a quote about what you studied, write down something someone in your family said while you were studying, have someone write their testimony about what you discussed, etc.)

Favorites:

Name	Favorite scripture, phrase or thing they learned today	Why they chose this

Goals: (What we can do to apply what we learned to our lives)

WHAT we are studying today

Date: _____   Time: _____   Place: _____

What is happening in our lives today:

_____

_____

_____

_____

In one sentence, today we are studying:

Things we need to understand before we read:
(background information)

What we learned: (Draw a picture, write a list of principles and doctrines you found, make a diagram, draw a map, make a family motto, write one word to sum up what you learned, find and write a quote about what you studied, write down something someone in your family said while you were studying, have someone write their testimony about what you discussed, etc.)

Favorites:

Name	Favorite scripture, phrase or thing they learned today	Why they chose this

Goals: (What we can do to apply what we learned to our lives)

WHAT we are studying today

Date: _____   Time: _____   Place: _____

What is happening in our lives today:

....

....

....

In one sentence, today we are studying:

Things we need to understand before we read:
(background information)

What we learned: (Draw a picture, write a list of principles and doctrines you found, make a diagram, draw a map, make a family motto, write one word to sum up what you learned, find and write a quote about what you studied, write down something someone in your family said while you were studying, have someone write their testimony about what you discussed, etc.)

Favorites:

Name	Favorite scripture, phrase or thing they learned today	Why they chose this

Goals: (What we can do to apply what we learned to our lives)

WHAT we are studying today

Date: _____   Time: _____   Place: _____

What is happening in our lives today:

_____

_____

_____

In one sentence, today we are studying:

Things we need to understand before we read:
(background information)

What we learned: (Draw a picture, write a list of principles and doctrines you found, make a diagram, draw a map, make a family motto, write one word to sum up what you learned, find and write a quote about what you studied, write down something someone in your family said while you were studying, have someone write their testimony about what you discussed, etc.)

Favorites:

Name	Favorite scripture, phrase or thing they learned today	Why they chose this

Goals: (What we can do to apply what we learned to our lives)

WHAT we are studying today

Date: _____   Time: _____   Place: _____

What is happening in our lives today:

_____

_____

_____

In one sentence, today we are studying:

Things we need to understand before we read:
(background information)

What we learned: (Draw a picture, write a list of principles and doctrines you found, make a diagram, draw a map, make a family motto, write one word to sum up what you learned, find and write a quote about what you studied, write down something someone in your family said while you were studying, have someone write their testimony about what you discussed, etc.)

Favorites:

Name	Favorite scripture, phrase or thing they learned today	Why they chose this

Goals: (What we can do to apply what we learned to our lives)

27

WHAT we are studying today

Date: _____   Time: _____   Place: _____

What is happening in our lives today:

_____

_____

_____

_____

In one sentence, today we are studying:

Things we need to understand before we read:
(background information)

What we learned: (Draw a picture, write a list of principles and doctrines you found, make a diagram, draw a map, make a family motto, write one word to sum up what you learned, find and write a quote about what you studied, write down something someone in your family said while you were studying, have someone write their testimony about what you discussed, etc.)

Favorites:

Name	Favorite scripture, phrase or thing they learned today	Why they chose this

Goals: (What we can do to apply what we learned to our lives)

WHAT we are studying today

Date: _____   Time: _____   Place: _____

What is happening in our lives today:

_____

_____

_____

In one sentence, today we are studying:

Things we need to understand before we read:
(background information)

What we learned: (Draw a picture, write a list of principles and doctrines you found, make a diagram, draw a map, make a family motto, write one word to sum up what you learned, find and write a quote about what you studied, write down something someone in your family said while you were studying, have someone write their testimony about what you discussed, etc.)

Favorites:

Name	Favorite scripture, phrase or thing they learned today	Why they chose this

Goals: (What we can do to apply what we learned to our lives)

WHAT we are studying today

Date: _____   **Time:** _____   **Place:** _____

What is happening in our lives today:

_____

_____

_____

In one sentence, today we are studying:

Things we need to understand before we read:
(background information)

What we learned: (Draw a picture, write a list of principles and doctrines you found, make a diagram, draw a map, make a family motto, write one word to sum up what you learned, find and write a quote about what you studied, write down something someone in your family said while you were studying, have someone write their testimony about what you discussed, etc.)

Favorites:

Name	Favorite scripture, phrase or thing they learned today	Why they chose this

Goals: (What we can do to apply what we learned to our lives)

WHAT we are studying today

Date: _____ **Time:** _____ **Place:** _____

What is happening in our lives today:

_____

_____

_____

In one sentence, today we are studying:

Things we need to understand before we read:
(background information)

What we learned: (Draw a picture, write a list of principles and doctrines you found, make a diagram, draw a map, make a family motto, write one word to sum up what you learned, find and write a quote about what you studied, write down something someone in your family said while you were studying, have someone write their testimony about what you discussed, etc.)

Favorites:

Name	Favorite scripture, phrase or thing they learned today	Why they chose this

Goals: (What we can do to apply what we learned to our lives)

WHAT we are studying today

Date: _____   Time: _____   Place: _____

What is happening in our lives today:

_____

_____

_____

In one sentence, today we are studying:

Things we need to understand before we read:
(background information)

What we learned: (Draw a picture, write a list of principles and doctrines you found, make a diagram, draw a map, make a family motto, write one word to sum up what you learned, find and write a quote about what you studied, write down something someone in your family said while you were studying, have someone write their testimony about what you discussed, etc.)

Favorites:

Name	Favorite scripture, phrase or thing they learned today	Why they chose this

Goals: (What we can do to apply what we learned to our lives)

WHAT we are studying today

Date: _____   Time: _____   Place: _____

What is happening in our lives today:

_____
_____
_____

In one sentence, today we are studying:

Things we need to understand before we read:
(background information)

What we learned: (Draw a picture, write a list of principles and doctrines you found, make a diagram, draw a map, make a family motto, write one word to sum up what you learned, find and write a quote about what you studied, write down something someone in your family said while you were studying, have someone write their testimony about what you discussed, etc.)

Favorites:

Name	Favorite scripture, phrase or thing they learned today	Why they chose this

Goals: (What we can do to apply what we learned to our lives)

WHAT we are studying today

Date: _____   **Time:** _____   **Place:** _____

What is happening in our lives today:

_____

_____

_____

In one sentence, today we are studying:

Things we need to understand before we read:
(background information)

What we learned: (Draw a picture, write a list of principles and doctrines you found, make a diagram, draw a map, make a family motto, write one word to sum up what you learned, find and write a quote about what you studied, write down something someone in your family said while you were studying, have someone write their testimony about what you discussed, etc.)

Favorites:

Name	Favorite scripture, phrase or thing they learned today	Why they chose this

Goals: (What we can do to apply what we learned to our lives)

WHAT we are studying today

Date: _____   Time: _____   Place: _____

What is happening in our lives today:

_____

_____

_____

In one sentence, today we are studying:

Things we need to understand before we read:
(background information)

What we learned: (Draw a picture, write a list of principles and doctrines you found, make a diagram, draw a map, make a family motto, write one word to sum up what you learned, find and write a quote about what you studied, write down something someone in your family said while you were studying, have someone write their testimony about what you discussed, etc.)

Favorites:

Name	Favorite scripture, phrase or thing they learned today	Why they chose this

Goals: (What we can do to apply what we learned to our lives)

WHAT we are studying today

Date: _____   Time: _____   Place: _____

What is happening in our lives today:

_____

_____

_____

In one sentence, today we are studying:

Things we need to understand before we read:
(background information)

What we learned: (Draw a picture, write a list of principles and doctrines you found, make a diagram, draw a map, make a family motto, write one word to sum up what you learned, find and write a quote about what you studied, write down something someone in your family said while you were studying, have someone write their testimony about what you discussed, etc.)

Favorites:

Name	Favorite scripture, phrase or thing they learned today	Why they chose this

Goals: (What we can do to apply what we learned to our lives)

WHAT we are studying today

Date: _____ Time: _____ Place: _____

What is happening in our lives today:

_____

_____

_____

In one sentence, today we are studying:

Things we need to understand before we read:
(background information)

What we learned: (Draw a picture, write a list of principles and doctrines you found, make a diagram, draw a map, make a family motto, write one word to sum up what you learned, find and write a quote about what you studied, write down something someone in your family said while you were studying, have someone write their testimony about what you discussed, etc.)

Favorites:

Name	Favorite scripture, phrase or thing they learned today	Why they chose this

Goals: (What we can do to apply what we learned to our lives)

WHAT we are studying today

Date: _____   **Time:** _____   **Place:** _____

What is happening in our lives today:

....

....

....

In one sentence, today we are studying:

Things we need to understand before we read:
(background information)

What we learned: (Draw a picture, write a list of principles and doctrines you found, make a diagram, draw a map, make a family motto, write one word to sum up what you learned, find and write a quote about what you studied, write down something someone in your family said while you were studying, have someone write their testimony about what you discussed, etc.)

Favorites:

Name	Favorite scripture, phrase or thing they learned today	Why they chose this

Goals: (What we can do to apply what we learned to our lives)

WHAT we are studying today

Date: _____   **Time:** _____   **Place:** _____

What is happening in our lives today:

....

....

....

In one sentence, today we are studying:

Things we need to understand before we read:
(background information)

What we learned: (Draw a picture, write a list of principles and doctrines you found, make a diagram, draw a map, make a family motto, write one word to sum up what you learned, find and write a quote about what you studied, write down something someone in your family said while you were studying, have someone write their testimony about what you discussed, etc.)

Favorites:

Name	Favorite scripture, phrase or thing they learned today	Why they chose this

Goals: (What we can do to apply what we learned to our lives)

WHAT we are studying today

Date: _____ Time: _____ Place: _____

What is happening in our lives today:

_____

_____

_____

In one sentence, today we are studying:

Things we need to understand before we read:
(background information)

What we learned: (Draw a picture, write a list of principles and doctrines you found, make a diagram, draw a map, make a family motto, write one word to sum up what you learned, find and write a quote about what you studied, write down something someone in your family said while you were studying, have someone write their testimony about what you discussed, etc.)

Favorites:

Name	Favorite scripture, phrase or thing they learned today	Why they chose this

Goals: (What we can do to apply what we learned to our lives)

WHAT we are studying today

Date: _____   Time: _____   Place: _____

What is happening in our lives today:

_____

_____

_____

In one sentence, today we are studying:

Things we need to understand before we read:
(background information)

What we learned: (Draw a picture, write a list of principles and doctrines you found, make a diagram, draw a map, make a family motto, write one word to sum up what you learned, find and write a quote about what you studied, write down something someone in your family said while you were studying, have someone write their testimony about what you discussed, etc.)

Favorites:

Name	Favorite scripture, phrase or thing they learned today	Why they chose this

Goals: (What we can do to apply what we learned to our lives)

55

WHAT we are studying today

Date: _____ Time: _____ Place: _____

What is happening in our lives today:

_____

_____

_____

In one sentence, today we are studying:

Things we need to understand before we read:
(background information)

What we learned: (Draw a picture, write a list of principles and doctrines you found, make a diagram, draw a map, make a family motto, write one word to sum up what you learned, find and write a quote about what you studied, write down something someone in your family said while you were studying, have someone write their testimony about what you discussed, etc.)

Favorites:

Name	Favorite scripture, phrase or thing they learned today	Why they chose this

Goals: (What we can do to apply what we learned to our lives)

WHAT we are studying today

Date: _____   Time: _____   Place: _____

What is happening in our lives today:

....

....

....

In one sentence, today we are studying:

Things we need to understand before we read:
(background information)

What we learned: (Draw a picture, write a list of principles and doctrines you found, make a diagram, draw a map, make a family motto, write one word to sum up what you learned, find and write a quote about what you studied, write down something someone in your family said while you were studying, have someone write their testimony about what you discussed, etc.)

Favorites:

Name	Favorite scripture, phrase or thing they learned today	Why they chose this

Goals: (What we can do to apply what we learned to our lives)

WHAT we are studying today

Date: _____   **Time:** _____   **Place:** _____

What is happening in our lives today:

_____

_____

_____

In one sentence, today we are studying:

Things we need to understand before we read:
(background information)

What we learned: (Draw a picture, write a list of principles and doctrines you found, make a diagram, draw a map, make a family motto, write one word to sum up what you learned, find and write a quote about what you studied, write down something someone in your family said while you were studying, have someone write their testimony about what you discussed, etc.)

Favorites:

Name	Favorite scripture, phrase or thing they learned today	Why they chose this

Goals: (What we can do to apply what we learned to our lives)

WHAT we are studying today

Date: _____   Time: _____   Place: _____

What is happening in our lives today:

....

....

....

In one sentence, today we are studying:

Things we need to understand before we read:
(background information)

What we learned: (Draw a picture, write a list of principles and doctrines you found, make a diagram, draw a map, make a family motto, write one word to sum up what you learned, find and write a quote about what you studied, write down something someone in your family said while you were studying, have someone write their testimony about what you discussed, etc.)

Favorites:

Name	Favorite scripture, phrase or thing they learned today	Why they chose this

Goals: (What we can do to apply what we learned to our lives)

WHAT we are studying today

Date: _____ Time: _____ Place: _____

What is happening in our lives today:

....

....

....

....

In one sentence, today we are studying:

Things we need to understand before we read:
(background information)

What we learned: (Draw a picture, write a list of principles and doctrines you found, make a diagram, draw a map, make a family motto, write one word to sum up what you learned, find and write a quote about what you studied, write down something someone in your family said while you were studying, have someone write their testimony about what you discussed, etc.)

Favorites:

Name	Favorite scripture, phrase or thing they learned today	Why they chose this

Goals: (What we can do to apply what we learned to our lives)

WHAT we are studying today

Date: _____ **Time:** _____ **Place:** _____

What is happening in our lives today:

_____

_____

_____

In one sentence, today we are studying:

Things we need to understand before we read:
(background information)

What we learned: (Draw a picture, write a list of principles and doctrines you found, make a diagram, draw a map, make a family motto, write one word to sum up what you learned, find and write a quote about what you studied, write down something someone in your family said while you were studying, have someone write their testimony about what you discussed, etc.)

Favorites:

Name	Favorite scripture, phrase or thing they learned today	Why they chose this

Goals: (What we can do to apply what we learned to our lives)

WHAT we are studying today

Date: _____   **Time:** _____   **Place:** _____

What is happening in our lives today:

_____

_____

_____

In one sentence, today we are studying:

Things we need to understand before we read:
(background information)

What we learned: (Draw a picture, write a list of principles and doctrines you found, make a diagram, draw a map, make a family motto, write one word to sum up what you learned, find and write a quote about what you studied, write down something someone in your family said while you were studying, have someone write their testimony about what you discussed, etc.)

Favorites:

Name	Favorite scripture, phrase or thing they learned today	Why they chose this

Goals: (What we can do to apply what we learned to our lives)

WHAT we are studying today

Date: _____   **Time:** _____   **Place:** _____

What is happening in our lives today:

_____

_____

_____

In one sentence, today we are studying:

Things we need to understand before we read:
(background information)

What we learned: (Draw a picture, write a list of principles and doctrines you found, make a diagram, draw a map, make a family motto, write one word to sum up what you learned, find and write a quote about what you studied, write down something someone in your family said while you were studying, have someone write their testimony about what you discussed, etc.)

Favorites:

Name	Favorite scripture, phrase or thing they learned today	Why they chose this

Goals: (What we can do to apply what we learned to our lives)

WHAT we are studying today

Date: _____   Time: _____   Place: _____

What is happening in our lives today:

....

....

....

In one sentence, today we are studying:

Things we need to understand before we read:
(background information)

What we learned: (Draw a picture, write a list of principles and doctrines you found, make a diagram, draw a map, make a family motto, write one word to sum up what you learned, find and write a quote about what you studied, write down something someone in your family said while you were studying, have someone write their testimony about what you discussed, etc.)

Favorites:

Name	Favorite scripture, phrase or thing they learned today	Why they chose this

Goals: (What we can do to apply what we learned to our lives)

WHAT we are studying today

Date: _____ Time: _____ Place: _____

What is happening in our lives today:

....

....

....

In one sentence, today we are studying:

Things we need to understand before we read:
(background information)

What we learned: (Draw a picture, write a list of principles and doctrines you found, make a diagram, draw a map, make a family motto, write one word to sum up what you learned, find and write a quote about what you studied, write down something someone in your family said while you were studying, have someone write their testimony about what you discussed, etc.)

Favorites:

Name	Favorite scripture, phrase or thing they learned today	Why they chose this

Goals: (What we can do to apply what we learned to our lives)

WHAT we are studying today

Date: _____   **Time:** _____   **Place:** _____

What is happening in our lives today:

_____

_____

_____

In one sentence, today we are studying:

Things we need to understand before we read:
(background information)

What we learned: (Draw a picture, write a list of principles and doctrines you found, make a diagram, draw a map, make a family motto, write one word to sum up what you learned, find and write a quote about what you studied, write down something someone in your family said while you were studying, have someone write their testimony about what you discussed, etc.)

Favorites:

Name	Favorite scripture, phrase or thing they learned today	Why they chose this

Goals: (What we can do to apply what we learned to our lives)

WHAT we are studying today

Date: _____   **Time:** _____   **Place:** _____

What is happening in our lives today:

_____

_____

_____

In one sentence, today we are studying:

Things we need to understand before we read:
(background information)

What we learned: (Draw a picture, write a list of principles and doctrines you found, make a diagram, draw a map, make a family motto, write one word to sum up what you learned, find and write a quote about what you studied, write down something someone in your family said while you were studying, have someone write their testimony about what you discussed, etc.)

Favorites:

Name	Favorite scripture, phrase or thing they learned today	Why they chose this

Goals: (What we can do to apply what we learned to our lives)

WHAT we are studying today

Date: _____ **Time:** _____ **Place:** _____

What is happening in our lives today:

_____

_____

_____

In one sentence, today we are studying:

Things we need to understand before we read:
(background information)

What we learned: (Draw a picture, write a list of principles and doctrines you found, make a diagram, draw a map, make a family motto, write one word to sum up what you learned, find and write a quote about what you studied, write down something someone in your family said while you were studying, have someone write their testimony about what you discussed, etc.)

Favorites:

Name	Favorite scripture, phrase or thing they learned today	Why they chose this

Goals: (What we can do to apply what we learned to our lives)

WHAT we are studying today

Date: _____   Time: _____   Place: _____

What is happening in our lives today:

....

....

....

In one sentence, today we are studying:

Things we need to understand before we read:
(background information)

What we learned: (Draw a picture, write a list of principles and doctrines you found, make a diagram, draw a map, make a family motto, write one word to sum up what you learned, find and write a quote about what you studied, write down something someone in your family said while you were studying, have someone write their testimony about what you discussed, etc.)

Favorites:

Name	Favorite scripture, phrase or thing they learned today	Why they chose this

Goals: (What we can do to apply what we learned to our lives)

WHAT we are studying today

Date: _____   Time: _____   Place: _____

What is happening in our lives today:

_____

_____

_____

In one sentence, today we are studying:

Things we need to understand before we read:
(background information)

What we learned: (Draw a picture, write a list of principles and doctrines you found, make a diagram, draw a map, make a family motto, write one word to sum up what you learned, find and write a quote about what you studied, write down something someone in your family said while you were studying, have someone write their testimony about what you discussed, etc.)

Favorites:

Name	Favorite scripture, phrase or thing they learned today	Why they chose this

Goals: (What we can do to apply what we learned to our lives)

WHAT we are studying today

Date: _____   Time: _____   Place: _____

What is happening in our lives today:

....

....

....

In one sentence, today we are studying:

Things we need to understand before we read:
(background information)

What we learned: (Draw a picture, write a list of principles and doctrines you found, make a diagram, draw a map, make a family motto, write one word to sum up what you learned, find and write a quote about what you studied, write down something someone in your family said while you were studying, have someone write their testimony about what you discussed, etc.)

Favorites:

Name	Favorite scripture, phrase or thing they learned today	Why they chose this

Goals: (What we can do to apply what we learned to our lives)

WHAT we are studying today

Date: _____   Time: _____   Place: _____

What is happening in our lives today:

_____

_____

_____

In one sentence, today we are studying:

Things we need to understand before we read:
(background information)

What we learned: (Draw a picture, write a list of principles and doctrines you found, make a diagram, draw a map, make a family motto, write one word to sum up what you learned, find and write a quote about what you studied, write down something someone in your family said while you were studying, have someone write their testimony about what you discussed, etc.)

Favorites:

Name	Favorite scripture, phrase or thing they learned today	Why they chose this

Goals: (What we can do to apply what we learned to our lives)

Favorites:

WHAT we are studying today

Date: _____   **Time:** _____   **Place:** _____

What is happening in our lives today:

_____

_____

_____

In one sentence, today we are studying:

Things we need to understand before we read:
(background information)

What we learned: (Draw a picture, write a list of principles and doctrines you found, make a diagram, draw a map, make a family motto, write one word to sum up what you learned, find and write a quote about what you studied, write down something someone in your family said while you were studying, have someone write their testimony about what you discussed, etc.)

Favorites:

Name	Favorite scripture, phrase or thing they learned today	Why they chose this

Goals: (What we can do to apply what we learned to our lives)

WHAT we are studying today

Date: _____   Time: _____   Place: _____

What is happening in our lives today:

_____

_____

_____

In one sentence, today we are studying:

Things we need to understand before we read:
(background information)

What we learned: (Draw a picture, write a list of principles and doctrines you found, make a diagram, draw a map, make a family motto, write one word to sum up what you learned, find and write a quote about what you studied, write down something someone in your family said while you were studying, have someone write their testimony about what you discussed, etc.)

Favorites:

Name	Favorite scripture, phrase or thing they learned today	Why they chose this

Goals: (What we can do to apply what we learned to our lives)

WHAT we are studying today

Date: _____   **Time:** _____   **Place:** _____

What is happening in our lives today:

_____

_____

_____

In one sentence, today we are studying:

Things we need to understand before we read:
(background information)

What we learned: (Draw a picture, write a list of principles and doctrines you found, make a diagram, draw a map, make a family motto, write one word to sum up what you learned, find and write a quote about what you studied, write down something someone in your family said while you were studying, have someone write their testimony about what you discussed, etc.)

Favorites:

Name	Favorite scripture, phrase or thing they learned today	Why they chose this

Goals: (What we can do to apply what we learned to our lives)

WHAT we are studying today

Date: _____   **Time:** _____   **Place:** _____

What is happening in our lives today:

_____

_____

_____

In one sentence, today we are studying:

Things we need to understand before we read:
(background information)

What we learned: (Draw a picture, write a list of principles and doctrines you found, make a diagram, draw a map, make a family motto, write one word to sum up what you learned, find and write a quote about what you studied, write down something someone in your family said while you were studying, have someone write their testimony about what you discussed, etc.)

Favorites:

Name	Favorite scripture, phrase or thing they learned today	Why they chose this

Goals: (What we can do to apply what we learned to our lives)

WHAT we are studying today

Date: _____   Time: _____   Place: _____

What is happening in our lives today:

_____

_____

_____

In one sentence, today we are studying:

Things we need to understand before we read:
(background information)

What we learned: (Draw a picture, write a list of principles and doctrines you found, make a diagram, draw a map, make a family motto, write one word to sum up what you learned, find and write a quote about what you studied, write down something someone in your family said while you were studying, have someone write their testimony about what you discussed, etc.)

Favorites:

Name	Favorite scripture, phrase or thing they learned today	Why they chose this

Goals: (What we can do to apply what we learned to our lives)

99

WHAT we are studying today

Date: _____   Time: _____   Place: _____

What is happening in our lives today:

_____

_____

_____

In one sentence, today we are studying:

Things we need to understand before we read:
(background information)

What we learned: (Draw a picture, write a list of principles and doctrines you found, make a diagram, draw a map, make a family motto, write one word to sum up what you learned, find and write a quote about what you studied, write down something someone in your family said while you were studying, have someone write their testimony about what you discussed, etc.)

Favorites:

Name	Favorite scripture, phrase or thing they learned today	Why they chose this

Goals: (What we can do to apply what we learned to our lives)

WHAT we are studying today

Date: _____ Time: _____ Place: _____

What is happening in our lives today:

_____

_____

_____

In one sentence, today we are studying:

Things we need to understand before we read:
(background information)

What we learned: (Draw a picture, write a list of principles and doctrines you found, make a diagram, draw a map, make a family motto, write one word to sum up what you learned, find and write a quote about what you studied, write down something someone in your family said while you were studying, have someone write their testimony about what you discussed, etc.)

Favorites:

Name	Favorite scripture, phrase or thing they learned today	Why they chose this

Goals: (What we can do to apply what we learned to our lives)

13954010R00055

Made in the USA
Charleston, SC
11 August 2012